PART 1



Before you watch

While you watch

After you watch

PART 2

# Benjy's fun

**1** Read.

## 2 Write the names.

## 3 Find the words.

| | | | | | |
|---|---|---|---|---|---|
| N | R | A | C | K | T |
| L | E | N | X | N | H |
| I | B | E | T | I | I |
| C | B | V | R | P | R |
| N | U | E | A | G | T |
| E | R | S | I | X | E |
| P | L | A | N | E | E |
| W | E | U | L | B | N |

## 4 Look at the pictures and do the crossword.

## 5 Write the words and find the message.

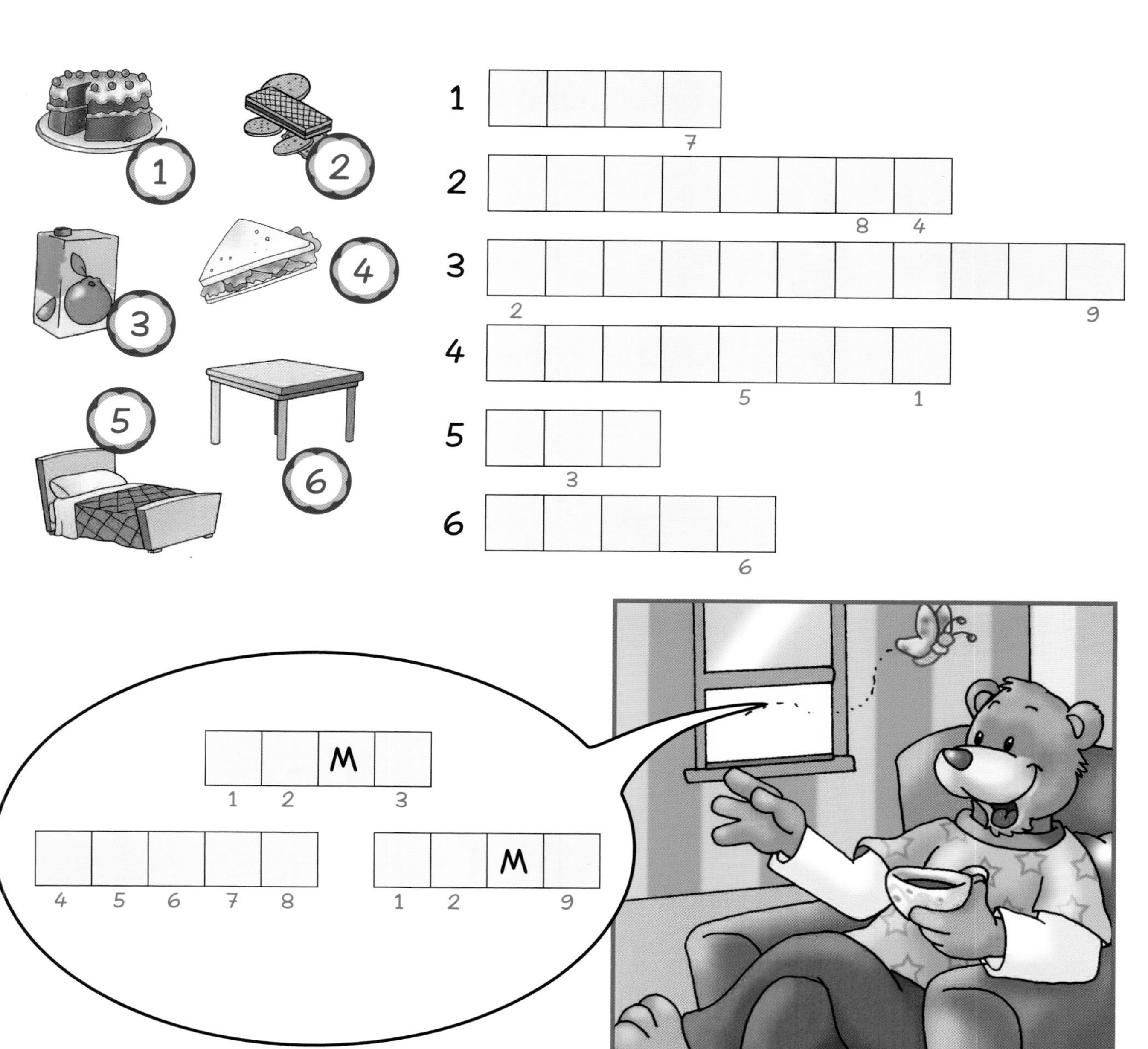


## 6 Tick the right word.

# Benjy's friends

**1** Look at the pictures and number the words.

| | | |
|---|---|---|
| (1) monster | ( ) ice-cream | ( ) pizza |
| ( ) four | ( ) football | ( ) red |
| ( ) green | ( ) fish | ( ) tennis |
| ( ) lollipops | ( ) dog | ( ) nine |
| ( ) ten | ( ) rabbit | ( ) picture |

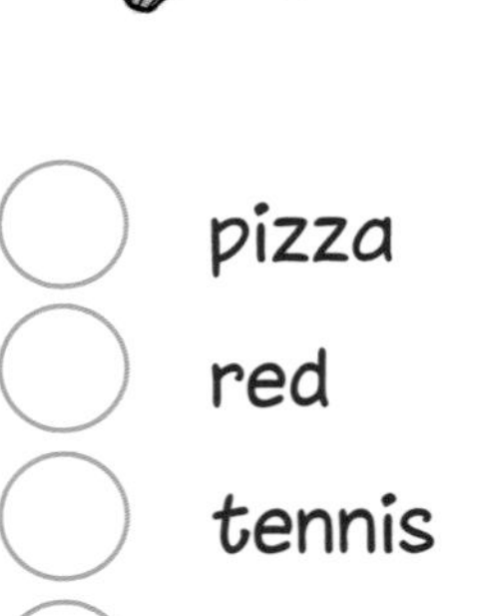

## 2 Read and match.

(3) I can play volleyball.
( ) I can't play the piano.
( ) I can't use the computer.
( ) I can draw a picture.

## 3 Look at the pictures and complete.

EDDY

I like green

I don't like yellow

I like ..........

I don't like ..........

JENNY

I like ..........

I don't like ..........

I like ..........

I don't like ..........

## 4 Listen and watch. Then read and complete.

red * piano * look * ~~monster~~ * friend * lollipops * pizza

My name is Benjy.

I'm 9 years old.

Benjy

My favourite colour is .......
My favourite food is ........
I like tennis.
I don't like ..................
I can paint a picture.
I can't play the .........

8

## 5 Tick true or false.

| | T | F |
|---|---|---|
| 1 I'm ten years old. | ✓ | ☐ |
| 2 My favourite colour is red. | ☐ | ☐ |
| 3 I like pizza. | ☐ | ☐ |
| 4 I don't like ice-cream. | ☐ | ☐ |
| 5 I can play tennis. | ☐ | ☐ |
| 6 I can't play the piano. | ☐ | ☐ |
| 7 I've got a cat. | ☐ | ☐ |

| | T | F |
|---|---|---|
| 1 I'm ten years old. | ☐ | ☐ |
| 2 My favourite colour is yellow. | ☐ | ☐ |
| 3 I like hamburgers. | ☐ | ☐ |
| 4 I don't like fish. | ☐ | ☐ |
| 5 I can play football. | ☐ | ☐ |
| 6 I can't use the computer. | ☐ | ☐ |
| 7 I've got a rabbit. | ☐ | ☐ |

**6** Complete your ID card.

- I'm ......................
- My favourite colour is ......................
- My favourite food is ......................
- My favourite animal is ......................
- I like ......................
- I don't like ..............
- I can ....................
- I can't ..................
- I've got .................

This is me.

**7** Draw your best friend and write his/her name.

# I'm afraid of...

## 1 Match.

1  spider / spiders  2

3  good night / good morning  4

5  bathroom / bedroom  6

7 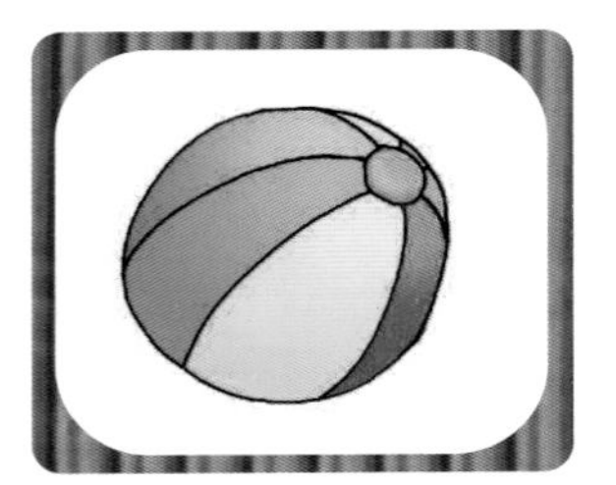 a big ball / a small ball  8

9  the dark / fire  10

11  monsters / monster  12

## 2 Look and complete.

## 3 Listen and watch. Then reorder the story.

2

What's the matter?
There's a spider.
7

A spider? Where is it?
It's in the bathroom.
8

Bye-bye!
9

Oh, it's a small spider!
10

I'm afraid of spiders.
Me, too!
11

## 4 Read and choose the correct sentence.

**1**

A Eddy says "Help me, please".

(B) Nick says "Help me, please".

C Jenny says "Help me, please".

**2**

A Benjy says "It's horrible".

B Eddy says "It's horrible".

C Nick says "It's horrible".

**3**

A Benjy is afraid of spiders.

B Nick and Molly are afraid of spiders.

C Molly isn't afraid of spiders.

**4**

A There's a spider in the bathroom.

B There's a spider in the bedroom.

C There isn't a spider in the bathroom.

**5**

A The spider is big.

B The spider isn't small.

C The spider is small.

**6**

A Molly says "Bye-bye".

B Jenny says "Bye-bye".

C Eddy says "Bye-bye".

## 5 Look at the chart and complete.

| |  |  |  |  |
|---|---|---|---|---|
| Sylvia | ✓ | | ✓ | |
| Alfred | | ✓ | | ✓ |
| Mary | | | ✓ | ✓ |
| John | ✓ | ✓ | | |

1 ........Sylvia........ is afraid of monsters and snakes.

2 ........................ is afraid of the dark and monsters.

3 ........................ is afraid of the dark and spiders.

4 ........................ is afraid of spiders and snakes.

5 ........................ and ........................ are not afraid of snakes.

6 ........................ and ........................ are not afraid of spiders.

7 ........................ and ........................ are not afraid of monsters.

8 ........................ and ........................ are not afraid of the dark.

## 6 Look at the pictures and do the crossword.

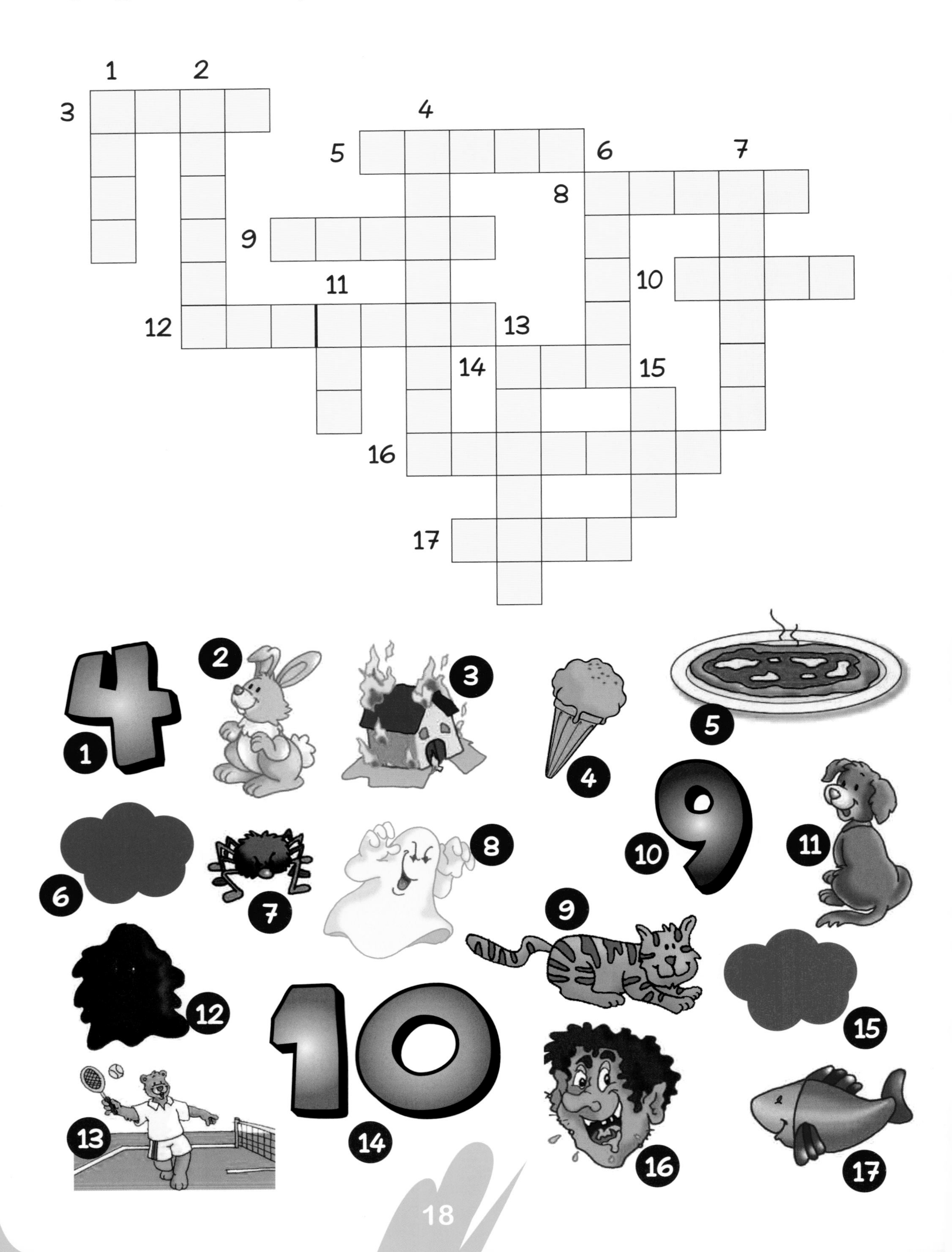

7 Play The Never-ending Sentences Game.

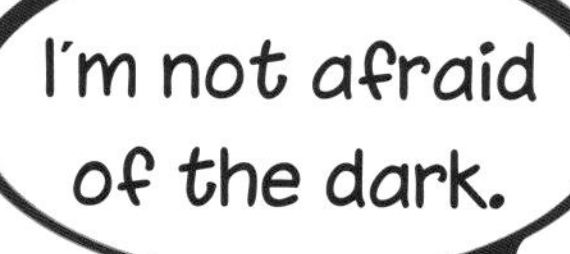


She's not afraid of the dark. I'm not afraid of fire.

She's not afraid of the dark. He's not afraid of fire. I'm not afraid of monsters.

# We like reading

## 1 Complete.

SPORTS BOOKS
ROMANCES
SCIENCE FICTION BOOKS
SCARY STORIES
THRILLERS
MYSTERY BOOKS
COMICS
WILDLIFE BOOKS

_ _ _ _ _ _

_ _ _ _ _ _ _ _ _ _ _ _ _ _ _ _ _ _ _ _ _ _

_ _ _ _ _ _ _ _ _ _ _ _ _ _ _ _ _ _ _ _ _ _

_ _ _ _ _ _ _ _ _ _ _ _ _ _ _ _ _ _

_ _ _ _ _ _ _ _ _ _ _ _ _ _ _ _ _ _ _ _ _ _ _ _ _ _ _ _ _ _ _ _ _

## 2 Read and complete.

1 Nick likes ..........................................

2 Eddy likes .................................., but he prefers ..........................

3 Jenny likes ..........................................

4 Molly prefers ..........................................

## 3 Write about you.

I like .................................., but I prefer ..........................

I don't like ..........................................

## 4 Listen and watch. Then find six mistakes.

Let's run away!
A giraffe!
6
Oh no, lions!
7
Quick! Climb up the house!
8
It's Benjy! Hurray!
Hold on to the rope.
9
Finally at home.
Thank you Benjy.
Bye-bye wild animals!
10

## 5 Read and choose the correct sentence.

**1**

(A) Molly likes scary stories.
B Molly doesn't like scary stories.
C Jenny likes scary stories.

**2**

A Nick doesn't like ghosts.
B Nick likes ghosts.
C Nick prefers scary stories.

**3**

A The children choose a comic.
B The children choose a sports book.
C The children choose a mystery book.

**4**

A The children see a grey rhino and three snakes.
B The children see a grey rhino and two snakes.
C The children see two grey rhinos and three snakes.

**5**

A The four friends go under a table.
B The four friends climb up a house.
C The four friends climb up a tree.

**6**

A Benjy helps the rhino.
B Benjy helps the children.
C Benjy climbs up the tree.

## 6 Match.

① I like Wildlife books. I usually read in the garden.

② I like Sports books. I usually read in the park.

③ I like Romances. I usually read in the living room.

④ I like Mystery books. I usually read in my bedroom.

a

b

c

d

# School life

## 1 Read and match the actions. Then write the names of the days of the week in the correct order.

Listen - Wednesday,
Stand up - Tuesday,
Hello - Monday,
Turn around - Friday,
Goodbye - Sunday,
Look - Thursday,
Sit down - Saturday.

Monday ______ ______ ______ ______ ______ ______

## 2 Write true or false.

1 It's six o'clock. [T]
2 It's seven o'clock. [ ]
3 It's eight o'clock. [ ]
4 It's ten o'clock. [ ]
5 It's two o'clock. [ ]
6 It's five o'clock. [ ]

## 3 Read and match.

1 

English

Science

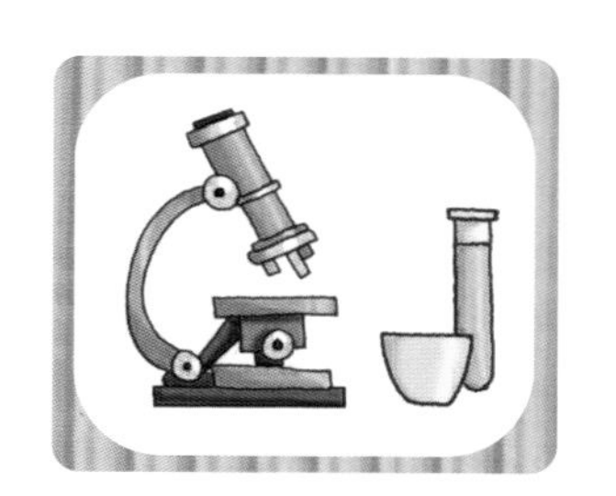 2

3 

Maths

Art

 4

5 

Geography

History

 6

7 

Music

P.E.

 8

## 4 Listen and watch. Then read and choose the correct words.

Here I am!
Benjy, I'm late and I can't find my foot / Maths Book?
7
Late?
Yes, Benjy, please, help me!
8
Here it is!
9
Bye-bye / Thank you Benjy!
10
11
Hello, Nick. Are you ready for our Sunday match / picnic?
12

## 5 Read and choose the correct sentence.

**1**

A It's eight o'clock.
B It isn't nine o'clock.
C It's nine o'clock.

**2**

A Nick has the Maths test today.
B Nick hasn't got the Maths test today.
C Nick has the Art test today.

**3**

A Benjy can't find his book.
B Nick can't find his book.
C Nick can find his book.

**4**

A Nick helps Benjy.
B Benjy helps Nick.
C Benjy doesn't help Nick.

**5**

A Benjy finds the book under the bed.
B Benjy finds the book under the table.
C Benjy doesn't find the book under the bed.

**6**

A There's no school on Monday.
B There's no school on Sunday.
C There's no test on Monday.

## 6 Match.

| Monday | Tuesday | Wednesday | Thursday | Friday |
|---|---|---|---|---|
| History | P.E. | Art | Computer Studies | English |
| Science | Maths | History | Geography | Art |

| Monday | Tuesday | Wednesday | Thursday | Friday |
|---|---|---|---|---|
| English | History | Maths | Science | Art |
| P.E. | Science | Geography | Music | Geography |

| Monday | Tuesday | Wednesday | Thursday | Friday |
|---|---|---|---|---|
| Science | Maths | P.E. | English | Maths |
| Geography | English | Art | History | P.E. |

1 Peter and Alan have English and P.E. on Monday.
2 ................. have Maths on Friday.
3 ................. have Geography on Wednesday and Music on Thursday.
4 ................. have Maths on Tuesday and on Friday.
5 ................. have History on Tuesday and Music on Thursday.
6 ................. have P.E. on Tuesday.

7 Look at the pictures and do the crossword.

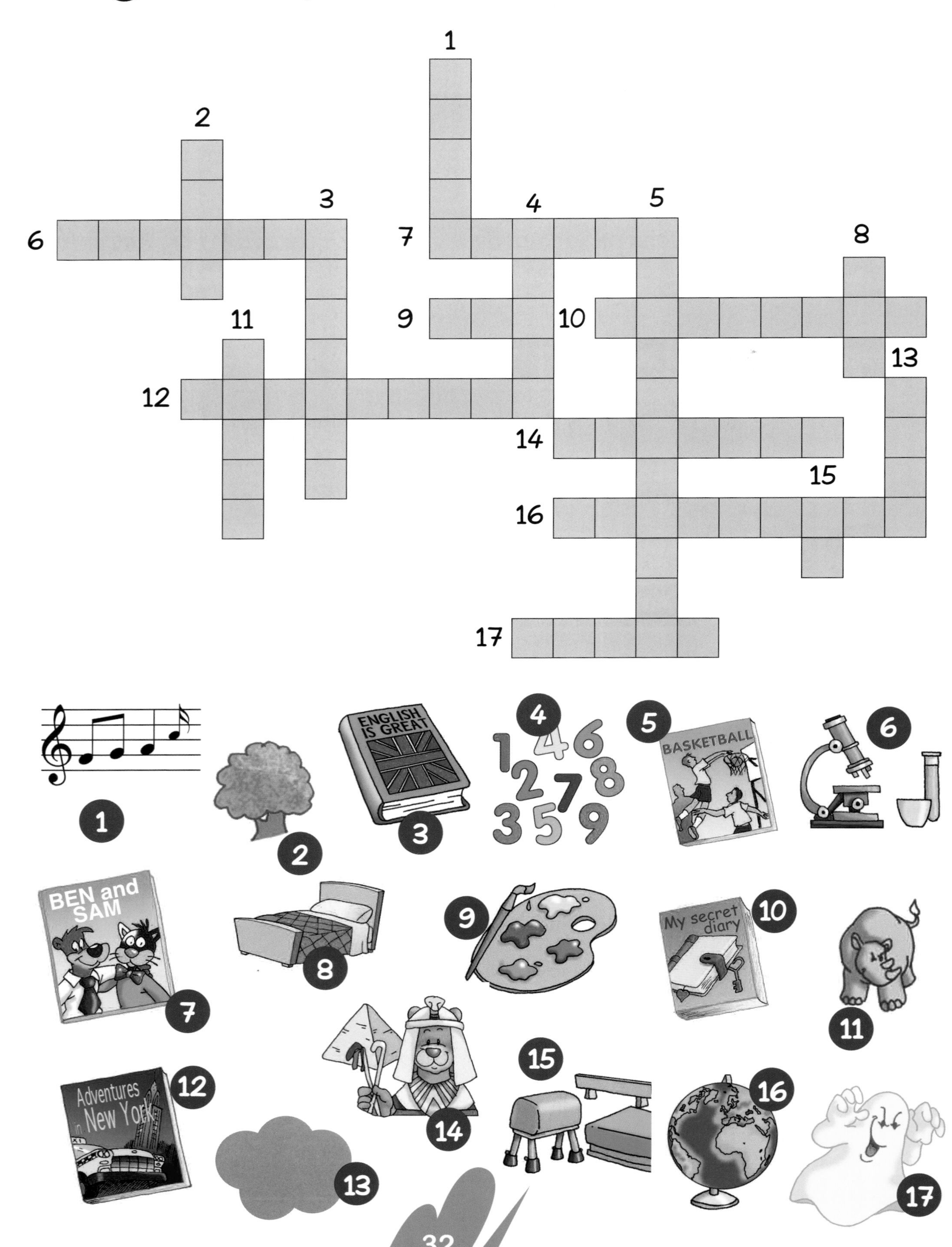

## 8 Play Guess the book I like.

# Shopping time

## 1 Complete.

toy shop | baker's | supermarket

~~pet shop~~ | book shop | clothes shop

the ..................

the ..................

the ..................

the ..................

the pet shop

the ..................

## 2 Answer the questions.

1 Where can you buy a T-shirt? At the clothes shop.
2 Where can you buy a cake? ..................
3 Where can you buy a skateboard? ..................
4 Where can you buy a tortoise? ..................
5 Where can you buy orange juice? ..................
6 Where can you buy a sports book? ..................

## 3 Match.

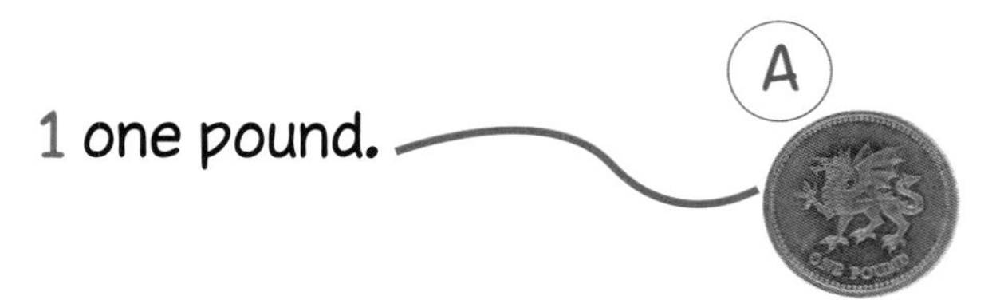

A B C D E F

1 one pound.

2 five pounds.

3 ten pounds.

4 fifteen pounds.

5 twenty pounds.

6 twenty-five pounds.

## 4 Count and answer.

1

How much is it?

2

How much is it?

## 5 Listen and watch. Then read and complete.

Here you are.
Thank you. Bye-bye.
6
At Benjy's house.
Where's B_ _ _ _ _?
You're right. Where is he?
7
Look! He's in the g _ _ _ _ _ _!
8
Hello friends! Welcome to my p _ _ _ _ _!
9
Do you like the decorations?
10

## 6 Read and choose the correct sentence.

**1**

A Benjy's birthday is tomorrow.
B Benjy's birthday is today.
C Benjy's birthday is in January.

**2**

A The children go to the supermarket.
B The children go to the baker's.
C The children go to the toy shop.

**3**

A The children buy a big cream cake.
B The children buy a big chocolate cake.
C The children buy a small cream cake.

**4**

A The cake costs twenty-five pounds.
B The cake costs five pounds.
C The cake costs fifteen pounds.

**5**

A Benjy is in the kitchen.
B Benjy isn't in the garden.
C Benjy is in the garden.

**6**

A In the garden there are many decorations.
B In the garden there are many toys.
C In the garden there are many children.

## 7 Read and act with your friends.

# The weather forecast

## 1 Complete.

| ~~snowy~~ | hot | cold | foggy | rainy |
|---|---|---|---|---|
| windy | cloudy | cool | warm | sunny |

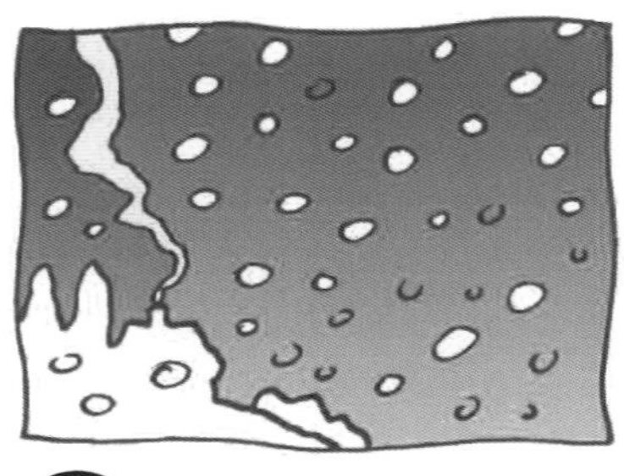

1 It's s n o w y.

2 It's _ _ _ N _

3 It's C _ _ _ _ _

4 It's _ U _ _ _

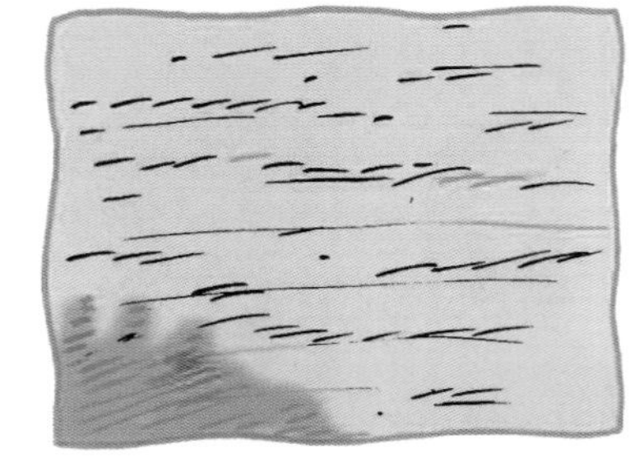

5 It's _ _ _ G _

6 It's _ I _ _ _

7 It's _ _ _

8 It's _ _ _ _

9 It's _ O _ _

10 It's _ _ _ D

## 2 Look and complete.

Winter

December

Spring

Summer

Autumn

What's the weather like today?

Today it's

## 3 Listen and watch. Then read and choose the correct words.

Let's try windy.
Oohh!
5
Rainy.
Stop it, please / thank you !
6
Ok, let's try snowy / sunny !
7
Oh, it's hot and beautiful!
8
Oh Benjy, your machine is wonderful / horrible !
9

## 4 Read and choose the correct sentence.

**1**

A Benjy's making a weather machine.

B Benjy's making a coffee machine.

C Benjy's making a time machine.

**2**

A Jenny asks "What's the weather like today?"

B Benjy answers "What's the weather like today?"

C Benjy asks "What's the weather like today?"

**3**

A Today it's snowy.

B Today it's cloudy.

C Today it's foggy.

**4**

A Nick and Molly don't like rainy weather.

B Nick and Jenny don't like snowy weather.

C Nick and Jenny don't like rainy weather.

**5**

A Nick and Jenny don't like sunny weather.

B Nick and Jenny like sunny weather.

C Nick and Jenny don't like hot weather.

**6**

A At the end of the story you can't see a camel.

B At the end of the story you can see a green camel.

C At the end of the story you can see a camel.

## 5 Read the sentences and write the month.

1. You celebrate St. Valentine's day.
February

2. Summer starts.
J..........

3. You can eat chocolate easter eggs
A..........

4. You open presents under the tree
D..........

5. It's the month before Christmas.
N..........

6. It's the first day of the year.
J..........

7. You start the new school year.
S..........

8. It's the last month of the holidays.
A..........

9. It's Halloween.
O..........

10. Spring starts.
M..........

11. It's name has got three letters.
M..........

12. You can leave for a long holiday.
J..........

It's my birthday. ..............................

**6** **Play** The weather forecast game.

**Key:**

It's windy.
Go forward three squares.

It's foggy.
You can't see. Miss a go.

It's cloudy.
Go back one square.

It's rainy.
Go back two squares.

It's sunny.
Have another go.

It's snowy.
Go back to "start".

# Detective story

## 1 Look and write the correct seasons.

Summer Spring Autumn Winter

1 ...............

2 ...............

3 ...............

4 ...............

## 2 Read and match.

1 In Winter
2 In Spring
3 In Summer
4 In Autumn

A it´s hot.
B it´s cold.
C it´s warm.
D it´s rainy and cloudy.

## 3 Complete.

| thief | Tutankhamun´s | glasses |
|---|---|---|
| thieves | plate | ring |

1 Two _ _ _ _ _ _ _ _

2 A _ _ _ _ _

3 A pair of _ _ _ _ _ _ _ _

4 A car number _ _ _ _ _

5 A _ _ _ _

6 _ _ _ _ _ _ _ _ _ _ _ _ _ `s mask

## 4 Listen and watch, then read and complete.

## 2 Complete.

Eddy likes watching
.......... programmes.

Jenny likes watching
.......... films.

Nick likes watching
.......... programmes.

Molly likes watching
.......... programmes.

Benjy likes watching
.......... films.

Nick's father likes watching
.............. .

## 3 Listen and watch. Then read and choose the correct word.

6
And we have to watch `Life in Australia´.
A nature / sport programme? Very interesting.
7
If you really want to see Australia, come with me.
8
9
In Australia you can find a lot of animals: cats / kangaroos, dingoes...
10
... and my Australian friends: koalas.
11

  **Watch the video, then tick the correct answer.**

1 Who switches on the TV?

Molly

Eddy

2 Does the TV work?

No, it doesn't.

Yes, it does.

3 Where do Benjy and the children go?

They go to school.

They go to Australia.

4 Which animals can you see at the end of the story?

Ants

Koalas

## 5 Look at the grids and tick true or false.

Lisa

| | | | |
|---|---|---|---|
| ✗ | ✗ | ♥ | ♥ |
| sometimes | never | always | often |

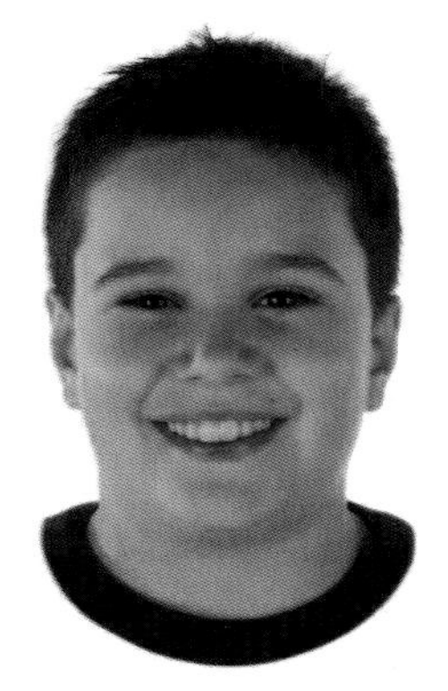
John

| | | | |
|---|---|---|---|
| ✗ | ♥ | ✗ | ♥ |
| sometimes | often | never | always |

| | T | F |
|---|---|---|
| 1 Lisa likes nature programmes. | ☐ | ☑ |
| 2 John likes music programmes. | ☐ | ☐ |
| 3 Lisa likes sport programmes. | ☐ | ☐ |
| 4 John likes romantic films. | ☐ | ☐ |
| 5 Lisa likes quiz shows. | ☐ | ☐ |
| 6 John likes detective films. | ☐ | ☐ |
| 7 Lisa likes science fiction films. | ☐ | ☐ |
| 8 John likes cartoons. | ☐ | ☐ |

# What's the matter?

**1** Look and tick the correct word.

1. tummy ache ☑ / backache ☐
2. backache ☐ / tummy ache ☐
3. backache ☐ / earache ☐
4. toothache ☐ / tummy ache ☐
5. earache ☐ / a headache ☐
6. a temperature ☐ / backache ☐
7. tummy ache ☐ / a cold ☐
8. a cough ☐ / earache ☐
9. backache ☐ / a sore throat ☐

## 2 Look at the pictures, then read and match.

1 Mum, I'm not very well. My back hurts.
2 I've got toothache!
3 Dad, my cat isn't very well.
4 The doctor says I need an injection.

A Let's go to the vet!
B Let's go to the doctor!
C Let's go to the dentist!
D Let's go to the nurse!

## 3 Listen and watch, then find six mistakes.

Hello, T.J.
You're my hero.
Oh... What's
the matter?
I've got a
cough.
7

Go and see
the dentist.
8

I'm afraid of
dentists.
Don't turn
around, come
with me.
9

OK.
Let's go!
10

Thank you, Eddy.
You're my doctor.
11

12

## 4 Watch the video, then tick the correct answer.

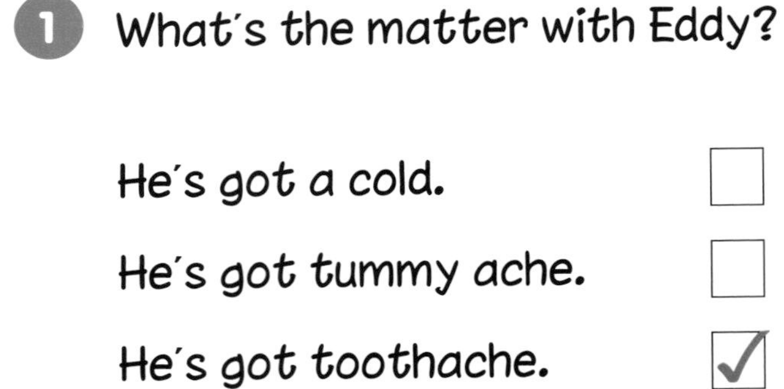

1 What's the matter with Eddy?

He's got a cold. ☐

He's got tummy ache. ☐

He's got toothache. ☑

2 Where do Molly and Eddy go?

They go to play basketball. ☐

They go to the dentist. ☐

They go to the vet. ☐

3 What is T.J. afraid of?

He's afraid of Eddy. ☐

He's afraid of ghosts. ☐

He's afraid of the dentist. ☐

## 5 Look, read and write the numbers.

## 6 Complete.

I want to be a musician

I want to be a ..............

I want to be a ..............

I want to be a ..............

## 7 Read and do the crossword.

1

2

3

4

5

6

7

8

9

ACROSS

4 Eddy and T.J. have got ..................

7 "Eddy, .................. on the TV, please."

8 Who goes to the dentist with Eddy and T.J.?

9 In Australia you can find kangaroos, dingoes and ..................

DOWN

1 "Watching this ........ programme is our homework for tomorrow."

2 "I've got toothache". "See the .................."

3 "Don't .................. . Come with me."

5 It's time to watch "Life in .................."

6 "Why are you so sad?" "Because the TV doesn't .................."

## 8 Find the words.
Use the remaining letters to complete the message.

| | | | | | | | | | | |
|---|---|---|---|---|---|---|---|---|---|---|
| T | E | M | P | E | R | A | T | U | R | E |
| N | A | T | U | R | E | A | C | O | L | D |
| N | A | B | A | C | K | A | C | H | E | T |
| U | R | C | A | R | T | O | O | N | E | P |
| S | O | R | E | T | H | R | O | A | T | R |
| C | O | U | G | H | O | M | U | S | I | C |
| G | S | P | O | R | T | S | R | A | M | M |
| D | E | T | E | C | T | I | V | E | E | V |
| R | O | M | A | N | T | I | C | E | R | Y |
| I | N | T | U | M | M | Y | A | C | H | E |
| T | O | O | T | H | A | C | H | E | T | E |
| T | H | E | N | E | W | S | R | E | S | T |
| H | E | A | D | A | C | H | E | I | N | G |

backache
cartoon
cold
cough
detective
headache
music
nature
romantic
sore throat
sports
the news
temperature
toothache
tummy ache

# Playing in the garden

**1 Put the pictures in the correct order and write the sentences.**

They're getting in their spaceship.

They're walking.

They're going to the moon.

They're putting on their helmets.

They're taking off.

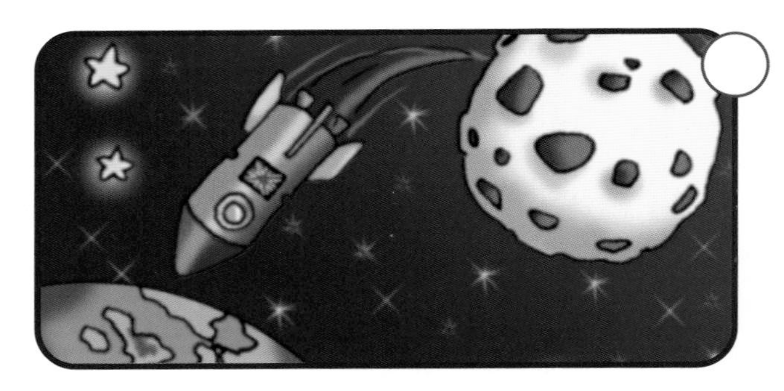

They're flying back.

1 They're putting on their helmets.
2 ...........................................................
3 ...........................................................
4 ...........................................................
5 ...........................................................
6 They're flying back.

## 2 Complete.

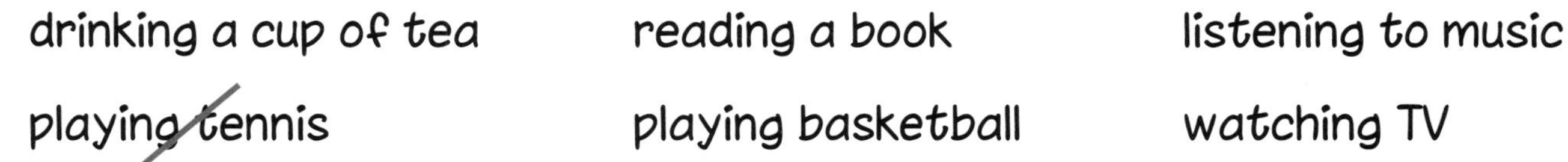

drinking a cup of tea — reading a book — listening to music

~~playing tennis~~ — playing basketball — watching TV

Nick and Eddy
are playing tennis.

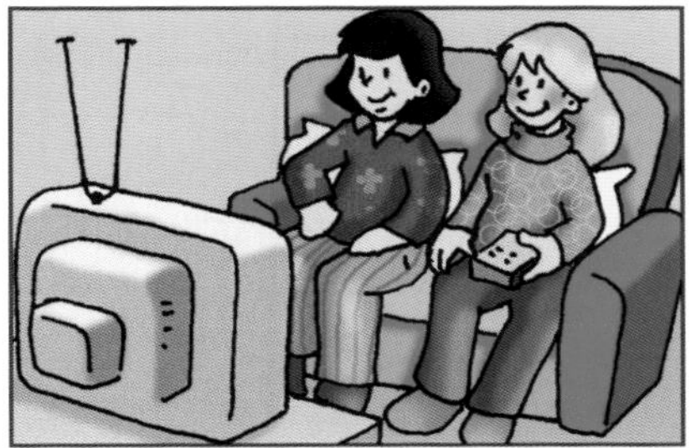

Jenny and Molly
are . . . . . . . . . . . . . . . . .

Eddy and Nick
are . . . . . . . . . . . . . . . . .

Molly
is . . . . . . . . . . . . . . . . .

Molly and Jenny
are . . . . . . . . . . . . . . . . .

Benjy
is . . . . . . . . . . . . . . . . .

## 3 Listen and watch, then read and complete.

Now finish the story.

10

## 4 Watch the video, then tick the correct answer.

1 What are Nick and Eddy making?

- They're playing basketball. ☐
- They're dancing. ☐
- They're making a spaceship. ☑

2 What does Jenny put on her head?

- A helmet. ☐
- A hat. ☐
- A scarf. ☐

3 What happens at the end of the story?

- They play tennis. ☐
- They take off. ☐
- They read a book. ☐

## 5 Read and write the names of the children. Then colour.

Alex is reading.
Paul is drinking.
Kevin is using the computer.
Sylvia is running.
Mary is eating.
Val is writing.

## 6 Complete and answer.

1 Who is reading a scary story? Alex

2 Who .............................. fruit juice? ..............

3 Who.............................. a sandwich? ..............

4 Who .............................. a letter? ..............

5 Who .............................. the computer? ..............

6 Who .............................. around the classroom? ..............

# Where I live

## 1 Complete.

station park statue greengrocer's library
bus stop post office swimming pool church

1

P_ _ _ O_ _ _ _ _

2

G_ _ _ _ _ _ _ _ _ _ ' _

3

S_ _ _ _ _

4

S_ _ _ _ _ _ _ _ P_ _ _

5

L_ _ _ _ _ _

6

P_ _ _

7

C_ _ _ _ _

8

B_ _ S_ _ _

9

S_ _ _ _ _ _

## 2 Read and do the crossword.

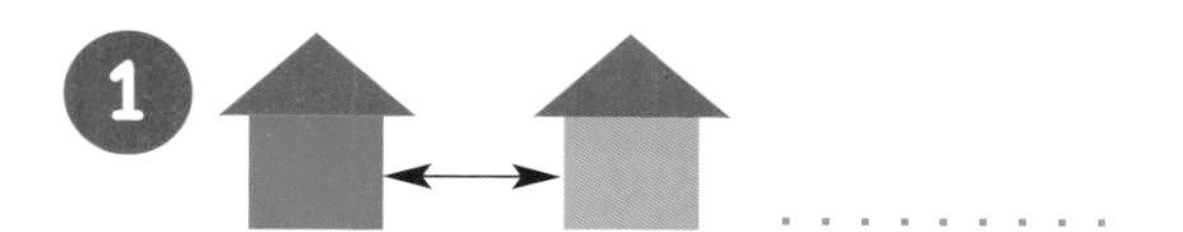


..........

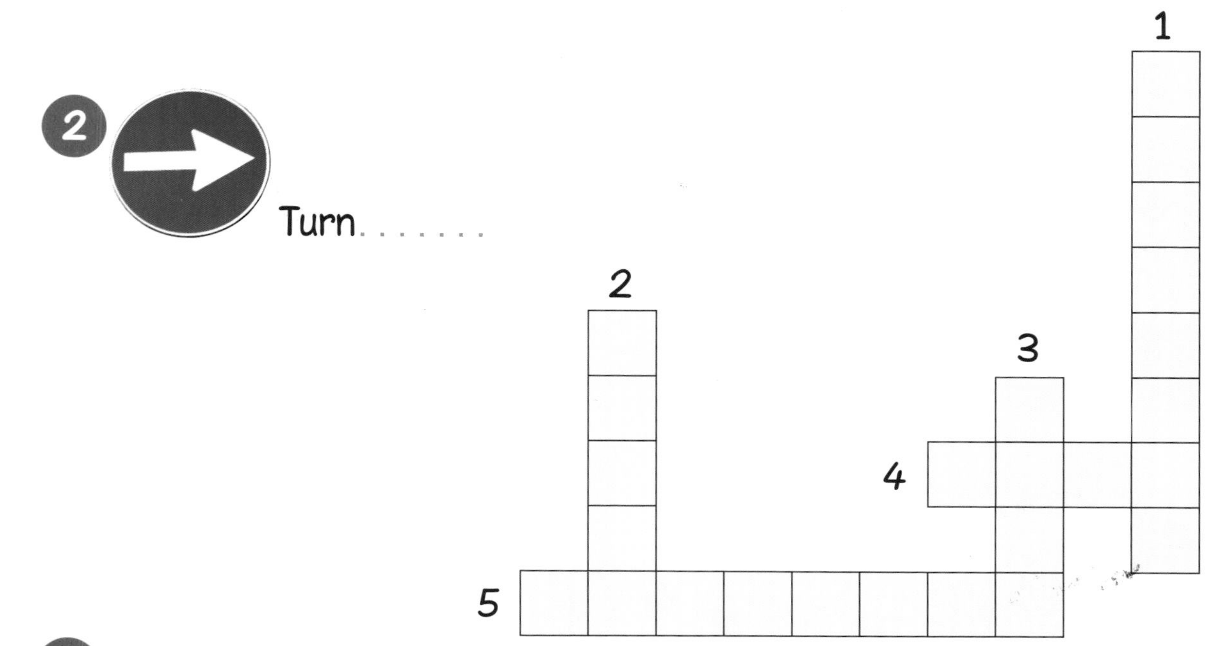


Turn........

Turn........

....... to

Go........on

## 3 Listen and watch, then reorder the story.

1

We must turn right.
6

POST OFFICE
COME INTO THE SHOP NEXT TO THE POST OFFICE
7

PET SHOP
Let's go in.
8

Welcome friends!
9

Benjy isn't here.
10

There's a message for us.
FOR MY FRIENDS: FOLLOW THE SIGNS
11

## 4 Watch the video, then tick the correct answer.

1. Where's Benjy?

- He's in the post office. ☐
- He's in the park. ☐
- He's in the snowball. ☑

2. Where is Benjy going?

- He is going to a concert. ☐
- He is going to the supermarket. ☐
- He is going to Nick's house. ☐

3. Where is the pet shop?

- It's in front of the post office. ☐
- It's next to the supermarket. ☐
- It's next to the post office. ☐

**5** You have to go to the library. Read and tick the correct information.

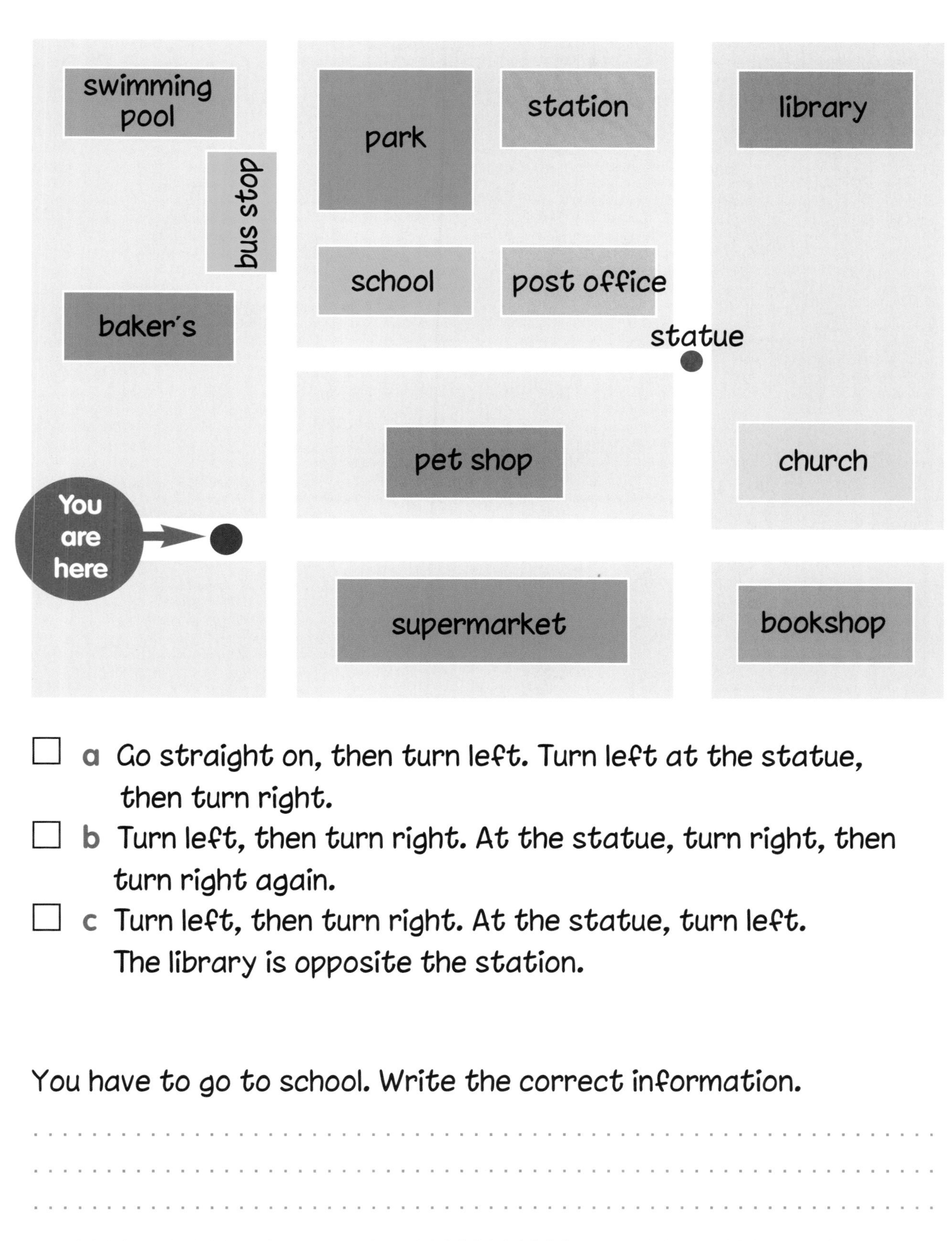


- ☐ **a** Go straight on, then turn left. Turn left at the statue, then turn right.
- ☐ **b** Turn left, then turn right. At the statue, turn right, then turn right again.
- ☐ **c** Turn left, then turn right. At the statue, turn left. The library is opposite the station.

You have to go to school. Write the correct information.

.....................................................................

.....................................................................

.....................................................................

.....................................................................

## 6 Look at the pictures and do the crossword.

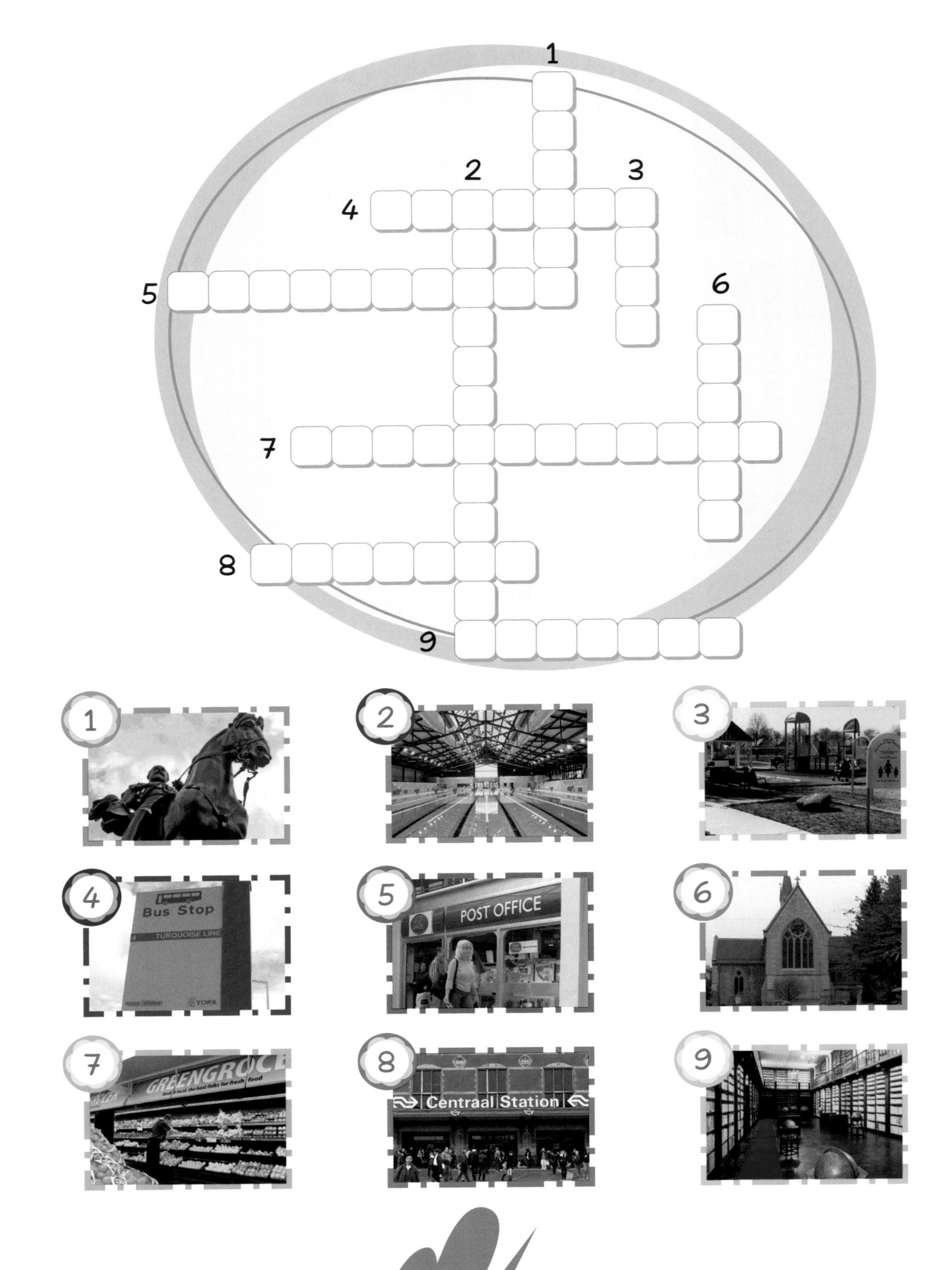

## 7 Find the words.
Use the remaining letters to complete the message.

| | | | | | | | | |
|---|---|---|---|---|---|---|---|---|
| S | P | A | C | E | S | H | I | P |
| P | A | R | K | T | M | O | O | N |
| L | I | S | T | E | N | I | N | G |
| O | P | L | A | Y | I | N | G | T |
| W | A | T | C | H | I | N | G | H |
| E | W | E | L | C | O | M | E | P |
| O | D | R | I | N | K | I | N | G |
| S | C | O | N | C | E | R | T | T |
| S | T | A | T | U | E | B | I | N |
| S | N | O | W | B | A | L | L | O |
| F | R | E | A | D | I | N | G | F |
| I | H | E | L | M | E | T | C | E |

bin
concert
drinking
helmet
listening
moon
park
playing
reading
snowball
spaceship
statue
watching
welcome

# Where are you from?

**1** Look and write about yourself.

Hello!
My name's Christine.
I'm from Canada.
I'm 11.
I speak English and French.

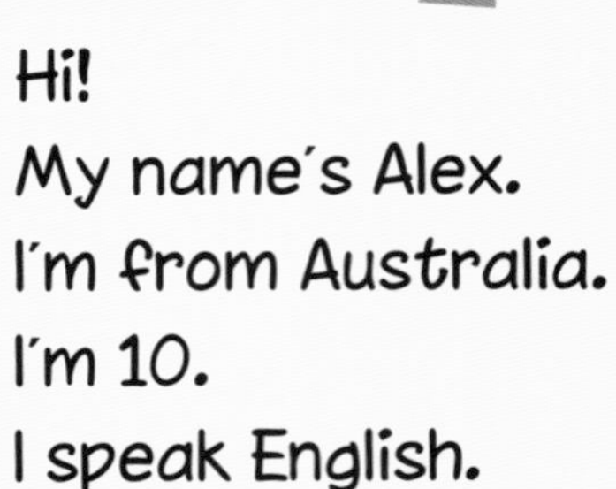

Hi!
My name's Alex.
I'm from Australia.
I'm 10.
I speak English.

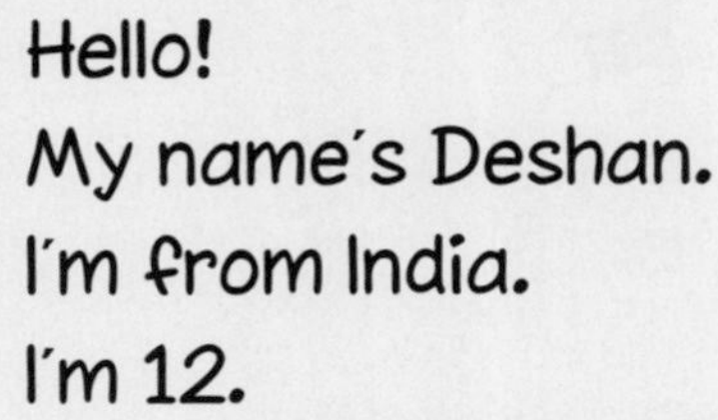

Hello!
My name's Deshan.
I'm from India.
I'm 12.
I speak Hindi and English.

## 2 Complete.

I'm from
The United Kingdom
Italy
Australia
The USA
Japan
Brazil

I'm
British
Italian
Australian
American
Japanese
Brazilian

I'm from ......
I'm .......

I'm from ......
I'm .......

I'm from ......
I'm .......

I'm from ......
I'm .......

I'm from ......
I'm .......

I'm from ......
I'm .......

## 3 Listen and watch. Then read and choose the right words.

Now finish the story.

12

## 4 Watch the video, then tick the correct answer.

1 Where is Alex from?

- He's from Canada. ☐
- He's from Australia. ☑
- He's from India. ☐

2 What is there in the garden?

- A bracelet. ☐
- A bicycle. ☐
- A kangaroo. ☐

3 What's the present?

- It's a bracelet. ☐
- It's a computer. ☐
- It's an e-mail. ☐

## 5 Look, read and complete.

Pierre's from ............................................ . He's French.

Maroula's from ............................................ . She's Greek.

Karl's from ............................................ . He's German.

Pedro and Fernando are from .......................... .They're Brazilian.

Maria and Anita are from .......................... .They're Spanish.

Chang's from ............................................ . He's Chinese.

Grazia and Paolo are from .......................... . They're Italian.

# NOTES